HOMEMADE FUDGE RECIPES

50+ EASY OLD FASHIONED DELICIOUS FUDGE IDEAS

COUNTRY SISTERS GOURMET

Country Sisters Gourmet. Copyright© 2014 by Alice Turner & CJ Vaughn. All rights reserved worldwide. No part of this book may be reproduced by any means whatsoever without the written permission from the authors.

All information in this book has been carefully researched and checked for factual accuracy. However, the authors and publisher make no warranty, express or implied, that the information contained herein is appropriate for every individual, situation or purpose, and assume no responsibility for errors or omissions. The reader assumes the risk and full responsibility for all actions, and the authors will not be held responsible for any loss or damage, whether consequential, incidental, special or otherwise that may result from the information presented in the publication.

We have relied on our own experience as well as many different sources for this book, and we have done our best to check facts and to give credit where it is due. In the event that any material is incorrect or has been used without proper permission, please contact us so that the oversight can be corrected.

Country Sisters Gourmet

ISBN-13: 978-1502428776
ISBN-10: 1502428776

Table of Contents

Fudge History	5
ALMOND JOY FUDGE	10
AMARETTO FUDGE	11
ANGEL FUDGE	12
APRICOT WHITE FUDGE	13
BISCOFF FUDGE	14
BLUEBERRY WHITE CHOCOLATE FUDGE	16
BUTTERSCOTCH FUDGE	17
CANDY BAR FUDGE	18
CANDY CANE CHRISTMAS FUDGE	19
CASHEW CHOCOLATE FUDGE	20
CHEESY PEANUT BUTTER FUDGE	21
CHEESECAKE FUDGE	22
CHERRY ALMOND WHITE CHOCOLATE FUDGE	23
CHERRY CHOCOLATE FUDGE	24
CHERRY VANILLA FUDGE	25
CHUNKY MALLOW FUDGE	26
COCONUT BUTTER FUDGE	27
COFFEE FUDGE	28
COOKIES N CREME WHITE CHOCOLATE FUDGE	29
CRACKER FUDGE	30
CRANBERRY FUDGE	31
EGGNOG WHITE CHOCOLATE FUDGE	32
FUDGE 1894	33
GRANDPAS FAMOUS PEANUT BUTTER FUDGE	34
GUMDROP WHITE CHOCOLATE FUDGE	35
IRISH CREAM FUDGE	36
KAHLUA FUDGE	37
LEMON FUDGE	38
MACA COCONUT FUDGE	39
MAPLE FUDGE	40
MILLION DOLLAR FUDGE	41
MINT CHOCOLATE FUDGE	42
ORANGE CHOCOLATE FUDGE	43
ORANGE N CREAM FUDGE	44
OREO FUDGE	46
PEANUT BUTTER FUDGE	47
PEANUT SOUR CREAM FUDGE	48
PECAN DATE FUDGE	49
PECAN PIE FUDGE	50
PANUCHE FUDGE	51
PINA COLADA FUDGE	52
PISTACHIO IRISH CREME FUDGE	53

PRALINE PECAN FUDGE	54
PUMPKIN FUDGE	55
RASPBERRY FUDGE BALLS	56
ROCKY ROAD FUDGE	57
SANTA'S WHITE FUDGE	58
SPICED PUMPKIN FUDGE	59
STRAWBERRY FUDGE	60
SUNSHINE LIME FUDGE	61
VANILLA FUDGE	62
WALNUT MAPLE FUDGE	63
About the Authors	65

Fudge History

Before 1886, the origin and history of fudge is unclear, but Fudge is thought to be an American invention. Most believe the first batch was a result of a accidental "fudged" batch of caramels, hence the name "fudge".

In 1886, fudge was sold at a local Baltimore grocery store for 40 cents a pound. This is the first known sale of fudge. A letter, found in the archives of Vasser College, written by Emelyn Battersby Hartridge reveals that Emelyn wrote that her schoolmate's cousin made fudge in 1886 in Baltimore and sold it for 40 cents a pound.

In 1888, Miss Hartridge asked for the fudge recipe, and made 30 pounds of fudge for the Vassar Senior Auction. The recipe was very popular at the school from that point forward. Fudge became a new confection after word spread to other women's colleges of the tasty delight. Later, Smith and Wellesley schools each developed their own recipe for fudge.

EASY GUIDES AND TIPS FOR COOKING YOUR CANDIES
Sugar and Other Sweeteners

Granulated sugar: If your recipe calls for "white sugar" or "sugar" it is referring to granulated sugar. The white sugar is made from sugarcane or sugar beets. I often use organic sugars (sugar in the raw) which is which has a light brownish color and seems to have a more flavorful taste and is easy to find in most stores. If you feel your recipe needs to be a pretty white sugary coating, use "white sugar".

Brown sugar: This sugar is granulated with added molasses and comes in either "light" or "dark". Light brown sugar has a milder flavor and is used more commonly in candy making. Brown sugars should not be used to replace other sugars. Brown sugar needs to be packed down in a measuring cup when measuring for a recipe. Brown sugars are simple to make, the recipe is included.

Superfine sugar: This sugar is also known as caster sugar in the old cookbooks. It is great for using in candy centers, because of its extra fine texture that dissolves quickly without the grainy texture of granulated sugars. You can use superfine sugars in place of regular granulated sugar with great results.

Powdered sugar: This sugar is commonly called confectioner's sugar and is used in many icing recipes. Powdered sugar is fine-textured sugar with cornstarch added. For best results, sift this sugar before adding it to recipes. Powdered sugar is easy to make, so I've included the recipe. I don't use this sugar unless called for in a recipe or to add a special decorated effect.

Corn syrup: This sweetener is also known as glucose and is made from cornstarch. It comes in "dark" and "light" varieties. I prefer the light for candy making. The corn syrup prevents other sugars from crystallizing and makes the candy firmer. It is used in fudges, cream fillings, and other candies.

Invert sugar: This sugar is known as liquid sugar. It is created by using a mixture of liquid (usually water) and white or brown sugar. The commercially produced versions commonly used are corn syrup or fructose. It's mostly used in making drinks, and it great for summer drinks like lemonade and iced coffee.

Honey: Any mild bee's honey can be used in recipes that call for honey. This honey should be in liquid form, and not the "creamed" or "honey spread" varieties.

Molasses: This is a by-product of the sugar refining process. It is a thick dark syrup with a distinctive flavor.

Eleven tests are considered for boiling sugar

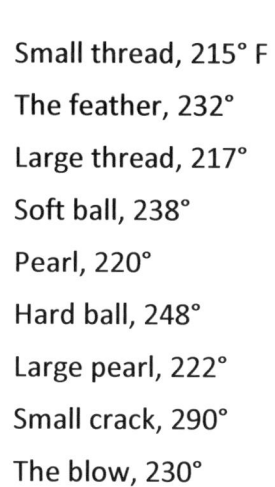

Small thread, 215° F

The feather, 232°

Large thread, 217°

Soft ball, 238°

Pearl, 220°

Hard ball, 248°

Large pearl, 222°

Small crack, 290°

The blow, 230°

Crack, 310°

Caramel, 350°

Now that you've been properly warned, here is a Candy Temperature reference table. Also check out the illustrated guide to candy temperature testing.

TIPS FOR PERFECT FUDGE

Fudge starts with sugar syrup, a solution of sugar in liquid. It can be a simple sugar and water combination or may contain other ingredients.

Always stir sugar and liquid over low heat {without boiling} until the sugar has completely dissolved.

If the mixture comes to the boil before all the sugar is dissolved, a crust of sugar crystals will form around the edge of the pan.

Brushing the pan. Take a small pastry brush and brush the sides of the pan to clean any crystals that might form during this starting phase. I've also taken a fork with a wet paper towel tightly wrapped around the tines and wiped the sides clean of any lingering sugars. DO NOT let any water drip into pan.

Once the sugar has completely dissolved, allow the mixture to come to a boil and DO NOT stir, unless specifically instructed to in the recipe. Stirring the boiling mixture will cause it to become crystallized and cloudy, which may or may not be desirable, depending on the recipe.

Using a candy thermometer is the easiest way in determining the fudge has reached the desired stage. A soft stage is reached at 155dC (249dF).

Boil the mixture for the full time as instructed in recipe. The candy thermometer should be fixed to the pan before the mixture comes to the boil.

When the candy thermometer reaches the temperature called for in the recipe, the fudge is ready. It's critical to watch the mixture carefully towards the end, because it will burn quickly if left cooking too long.

The length of time the mixture cooks, and the temperature it reaches in that given time, determines how the mixture will set.

If you don't have a candy thermometer, fudge is a forgiving mixture. You can use the cold water test.

Another way to check for soft-ball stage is to drop a small amount of mixture into a shallow cup of very cold water. It should form a soft ball when rolled between your thumb and finger.

Use a long-handled wooden spoon if the mixture is to be stirred while still hot. The wood will not conduct heat.

As soon as the mixture is ready remove the pan from the heat. Be careful because the pan will be very hot.

BEATING THE MIXTURE

Depending on the recipe, the mixture may be beaten while still hot, or you may have to wait until it has cooled. Beating thickens the mixture and causes it to lose its gloss. The recipe will indicate whether to use a wooden spoon or electric beaters - it is not a good idea to use electric beaters in a very hot mixture. There is usually a fine line between the mixture reaching the desired consistency and being too firm and dry to spread into the tin, so watch it carefully as you work.

Note: We used a silicone pan and it made popping the fudge out so easy!

~~WARNING~~
A Word of Caution

PLEASE - BE CAREFUL when working with hot sugar, especially if you decide to use the cold-water method of temperature testing. Sugar burns are nasty. Hot sugar is almost impossible to quick rub or rinse off the skin, and thus continues burning long after it comes into contact with your skin. DO NOT ALLOW CHILDREN TO HELP YOU WHILE THIS HOT STAGE OF COOKING. If burned... hold under cold water to wash off sugar mixture and continue to keep burn immersed in cold water for another 10 min. Please do not allow yourself to be careless or become distracted when working with hot sugar. Avoid dangling hair, jewelry, clothing, and children near the work area. Always use a long-handled wooden spoon for stirring and beating. Be extra careful if using electric beaters with the hot sugar to not sling this hot mixture out of the bowl.

ALMOND JOY FUDGE

2 (12 oz) packages **chocolate chips**
2 (14 oz) cans **sweetened condensed milk**
2 tsp **vanilla extract**
2 cups **mini almond joy candy bars**, cut into 1/2 inch pieces (16)

Time - 20 min.

Butter an 8" square baking pan and line with wax paper to overhang two sides by 2 inches.

In pan, combine **chocolate chips and condensed milk** over medium heat and cook, stirring constantly until melted& smooth.

Remove from heat and stir in **vanilla and candy bars**. Spread mixture evenly in pan.

Refrigerate until firm for at least 2 hours.

Use wax paper to help remove from pan. Approximately 36 squares.

AMARETTO FUDGE

3 cups **chocolate chips**
1 can (14 ounces) **sweetened condensed milk**
1/2 tsp **vanilla extract**
2 tbsp **Amaretto Liquor** (Substitute **1 tsp almond extract**)
1/2 cup **sliced toasted almonds**

Time - 30 min. + cooling

Line a 9x9" or an 8x8" pan with foil and spray with **cooking spray**.

Toast almonds, place on a cookie sheet and bake at **350 degrees for just a 1-2 minutes**, stirring occasionally. DO NOT burn.

Mix **chocolate chips and sweetened condensed milk** in a medium saucepan. Stirring on LOW heat until melted, stirring occasionally. When **chocolate chips** are melted, remove heat, and stir in **vanilla and Amaretto.**

Quickly spread in prepared pan. Sprinkle with **toasted almonds**. Press with spoon to set almonds in fudge. Cool at room temperature, chill until hardened.

ANGEL FUDGE

2 cups **sugar**
1 cup **milk**
1 cup **Hershey's chocolate syrup**
1 tbsp **butter**
1 tsp **vanilla**
3/4 cup **marshmallow crème**
Chopped nuts (optional)

Time - 20 min.

Butter 8 inch square pan, or a cookie sheet.

In heavy 3 quart saucepan, combine **sugar, milk and syrup**. Cook over medium heat, stirring constantly until well blended. Continue to cook without stirring to **234 degrees** or until syrup, when dropped into very cold water, forms a soft ball which flattens when removed from water.

Bulb of candy thermometer should not rest on bottom of saucepan.

Remove from heat. Add **butter, vanilla and marshmallow crème**. Do not stir.

Cool at room temperature. Beat with wooden spoon until fudge loses gloss [fudge will hold shape]. Quickly spread into prepared pan

Cool – Cut into squares. Makes 3 dozen.

APRICOT WHITE FUDGE

1-1/2 tsp plus 1/2 cup **butter**, divided
2 cups **sugar**
3/4 cup **sour cream**
12 ounces **white baking chocolate**, chopped
1 jar (7 ounces) **marshmallow creme**
3/4 cup chopped **dried apricots**
3/4 cup chopped **walnuts**

Time - 15 min. + cooling

Grease 9 in pan with 1 1/2 tsp butter set aside.

In heavy saucepan, combine **sugar, sour cream and remaining butter**. Bring to a boil over medium heat, stirring constantly. Cook and stir until a candy thermometer reads 234° (soft-ball stage), about 5-1/2 minutes.

Remove from the heat. Stir in **chocolate** until melted. Stir in **marshmallow creme** until blended. Fold in **apricots and walnuts**. Pour into prepared pan.

Cover and refrigerate overnight. Using foil, lift fudge out of pan. Discard foil; cut fudge into
squares.

Yield: about 2 pounds.

BISCOFF FUDGE

3 cups **powdered sugar**
1 cup **Biscoff butter**
2 1/2 cups **brown sugar**
1/2 cup **butter**
2 tsp **vanilla extract**
3/4 cup **milk**
2 tsp **cinnamon**
2 tsp **nutmeg**
1 tsp **ground cloves**

Time - 30 min. + cooling

Grease an 8x8 pan with cooking spray or butter. Set aside.

Measure **powdered sugar** in large bowl. Set aside.

Melt **butter** to a medium saucepan. Add **brown sugar and milk**, stirring to combine as you bring to a boil.

Once mixture is boiling, cook for 1 minute, stirring and scraping bottom continuously. Careful not to burn. Lower heat, add **vanilla and Biscoff butter**, stirring until butter is dissolved, smooth and creamy.

Remove from heat and quickly add it to your **powdered sugar, mixing on medium quickly** with a hand-mixer. As soon as everything is combined, pour into buttered pan. Smooth with spatula.

Cover with plastic wrap and store in refrigerator 1+ hours. Remove from pan and cut into small pieces. Store in air tight container in refrigerator. Serve room temperature.

NOTE: Biscoff spread is a peanut butter-like spread made of speculoos cookies. Speculoos are buttery, brown sugar and spice-flavored cookies that are similar to gingersnaps and are popular in the Netherlands. The smooth and creamy spread is made into a thick spread with the addition of sugar, vegetable oil, deep brown sugar, butter and spice flavor to it.

The spread isn't available at all grocery stores, but many are starting to carry it. Trader Joe's recently started carrying it, packaged as Speculoos Cookie Butter, plus specialty stores and online.

BLOND SILK FUDGE

1/4 cup **butter**
3 oz **unsweetened chocolate**
1 pound **confectioner's sugar (powdered)**
1/3 **dry milk**
1/2 cup **light corn syrup**
1 tbsp **water**
1 tsp **vanilla extract** (or use your favorite extract, mint and orange are good)
1/2 to 1 cup **Chopped nuts**(optional)

Time - 25 min.

Butter an 8" square pan, or spray a cookie sheet with non-stick spray.

Sift together **powdered sugar and powdered milk**. In a double boiler, (over boiling water), melt together **butter and chocolate**, then stir in **corn syrup, water** and **vanilla.**

Remove from heat, and pour into pan. Cool and cut into squares.

BLUEBERRY WHITE CHOCOLATE FUDGE

3 cups of **cane sugar**
1 1/2 sticks of **butter**
2/3 cups of **evaporated milk**
12 oz of **white chocolate chips**
1 - 7.5 ounce jar of **marshmallow cream**
2 tsp of **vanilla**
2 cups of **dried blueberries**

Time - 30 min. + cooling

Melt **butter, sugar and evaporated milk** until smooth. Bring to rolling boil over medium heat stirring constantly to reach **soft ball stage (235 F)**. for 3-5 minutes.

Remove pan from heat, stir in **marshmallow cream** until smooth. (Warm marshmallow cream by placing in microwave 20-30 seconds to remove marshmallow easily.) Add **white chocolate** and stir until melted and smooth. **White chocolate is easily burned**. Do not reach a brown color! Watch carefully. Add **vanilla and blueberries,** stir to mix.

Pour **white chocolate/blueberry mixture** into a **13 X 9 inch pan** that has been buttered liberally and spread to the corners of pan with spoon. Cool to room temperature, cut into small squares.

This fudge can be stored in the fridge or even freezer if you want until you are ready to use it. It will last about a week at room temperature in air tight container.

You can add in other dried berries. Dried cranberry, dried cherry, or Goji berries are good.

BUTTERSCOTCH FUDGE

1 cup **chopped pecans**
3 cups **butterscotch chips**
1 tbsp **butter**
1 can (14 ounces) **sweetened condensed milk**
1 tsp **vanilla extract**
1/4 tsp **sea salt** (or kosher salt)

Time - 45 min. + cooling

Line a 9"x9" pan with foil and spray with **cooking spray.**

Toast your **pecans** in a small frying pan over low heat. Stir continuously for a minute, not to burn. When you smell them, remove heat and place on cookie sheet to cool.

Combine **butterscotch chips, butter, and sweetened condensed milk** in a medium saucepan over **low heat. Melt ingredients** together, continuing to stir.

Once the **butterscotch, butter, and milk are melted together**, remove from heat and stir in **vanilla and pecans.**

Pour into **prepared pan**. Sprinkle with **salt** while still hot. Cool to room temperature, then refrigerate until firm. Store in air tight container.

CANDY BAR FUDGE

1 cup **semisweet chocolate chips**
1 cup **butterscotch chips**
1 can **Pillsbury creamy supreme milk chocolate frosting**
2 **Snickers or Heath candy bars**, chopped

Time - 15 min.

Line 8-inch square pan with foil, extending foil over the edges; **lightly grease** foil.

Melt **chips** in microwave on high for 1 to 2 minutes, stirring occasionally, until melted.

Stir in **frosting and all but 2 Tbsp. of the candy bars**; blend well.

Spread in foil-lined pan and sprinkle with reserved candy. Refrigerate 1 hour or firm.

Remove fudge from pan by lifting foil out. Remove foil from fudge, cut into squares.

CANDY CANE CHRISTMAS FUDGE

2 (10 ounce) packages **vanilla baking chips (or white baking morsels)**
14 oz **sweetened condensed milk**
3/4-1 tsp **peppermint extract** (depending on preferences)
1 1/2 cups **finely-crushed candy canes**
red food coloring

Time - 25 min.

Line an 8x8-inch square baking pan with aluminum foil. Lightly coat the bottom of the foil with **butter**.

In a medium size saucepan, combine the **vanilla chips** and the **sweetened condensed milk**. Cook over medium heat, stirring frequently, until the **vanilla chips are melted**.

Remove the pan from the heat and continue to stir (to remove any lumps that might be left from partially unmelted chips).

When chips are completely melted, stir in the **peppermint extract and crushed candy canes**.

Spread the fudge mixture evenly in the bottom of the prepared baking pan.

Dot the top of the fudge with several drops of food coloring (I use about 10 drops of food coloring). Reduce or increase that, depending on the amount of swirling you wish in your fudge. With a butter knife, cut through the fudge and food coloring, making a swirling pattern throughout the fudge.

Chill for 2 hours. Remove the fudge from the baking pan by lifting the foil from both ends. Cut fudge into 1-inch squares.

CASHEW CHOCOLATE FUDGE

4 1/2 cups **sugar**
1 12 oz can **evaporated milk**
2 cubes **butte**r (2 sticks, 1/2 cup each)
2 12 oz bags **White Chocolate Chips**
7 oz jar **marshmallow cream**
2 tsp **vanilla**
6-9 oz **salted cashews**

Time - 30 min.

Mix in mixing bowl, **white chocolate chips, marshmallow cream, vanilla, and 1 cube of butter**.

In medium saucepan, combine **butter, sugar and evaporated milk**. Bring to a boil on medium high heat and let it boil for 10 minutes, stirring continually.

Pour **hot syrup** over **chocolate chips, marshmallow cream, butter, and vanilla,** whip in mixing bowl until well mixed.

Pour mixture into a 9X13 dish with **waxed paper sprayed with cooking spray.**

Evenly spread the **cashews** on top making sure they won't come out of fudge when it is flipped. Place in refrigerator to set.

When you are going to cut, flip over on cutting board and cut them into squares. Store in air tight container in refrigerator.

CHEESY PEANUT BUTTER FUDGE

1/2 lb **Velveeta cheese**, sliced
1 cup **butter** (2 sticks)
1 cup **creamy peanut butter**
1 tsp **vanilla extract**
1 cup **chopped nuts**
1(16 ounce) bag **confectioners sugar**

Time - 40 min. + cooling

Spray bottom of a 9 by 2-inch square pan with **butter nonstick cooking spray**.

Melt **cheese and butter together** in medium sauce pan over medium heat. Add **peanut butter**
stirring until smooth. Remove heat, add **vanilla and nuts.**

Add **confectioners sugar** into a large bowl, pour **cheese mixture over sugar**. Stirring until mixed. Candy will be stiff.

Using your hands, **remove candy** from the bowl and press evenly and firmly into the pan.

Remove excess **butter** (oil) from top of candy by patting with paper towel.

Firm in refrigerator. Cut into squares.

(We got this recipe from a magazine several years back from Paula Deen.)

CHEESECAKE FUDGE

2 cups **flour**
8 oz **cream cheese**, cut up
2/3 cup **brown sugar**, packed
2 **eggs**
1 1/2 cups **butter**, cut up
3/4 cup **slivered almonds**
1 pkg. creamy **Chocolate Fudge Frosting mix** for 2 layer cake

Time - 35 min.

Combine **flour, butter and brown sugar** in large bowl. Beat with electric mixer on low until **butter** is cut into dry ingredients. (Pastry blender may be used.)

Place this mixture into an ungreased 13 x 9 x 2-inch pan. **Bake at 350 degrees** for **10 to 12 minutes**.

Meanwhile, **mix frosting and cream cheese** until combined. Add **eggs** and beat until smooth. Carefully spread **chocolate mixture** over hot crust. Sprinkle with almonds. Bake at **350 degrees for 30 minutes** or until chocolate mixture is set.

Cool. Cut into bars and store in refrigerator. Makes 32.

CHERRY ALMOND WHITE CHOCOLATE FUDGE

1 1/2 cups **sugar**
2/3 cup **milk**
1/4 cup **butter**
1 1/2 cups **white chocolate chips**
1 tsp **vanilla**
1/2 cup sliced **almonds**, toasted
1/2 cup **dried cherries**

Time - 30 min.

Line a 8" square pan with foil. Spray **buttered non-stick** on foil.

Mix **sugar and milk** in a heavy 3 quart saucepan. Add **butter** and bring to a boil over med. heat, stirring constantly without stirring, boil vigorously 5 min.

Remove from heat. Add **chips and vanilla**. Stir, whisk until chips melt and mixture is smooth. Stir in **almonds and cherries**.

Spread in prepared pan. Refrigerate 6 hours or until firm.

CHERRY CHOCOLATE FUDGE

1 cup **sugar**
2 tbsp **butter**
1/4 tsp **salt**
1/3 cup **half-and-half milk**
1 cup miniature **marshmallow**
1 cup **cherry chips**
1 cup **chocolate chips**
1/2 cup **peanut butter**
1 cup **salted peanuts**

Time- 35 min.

Combine **sugar, butter, salt and half and half** in saucepan. Boil on high heat for about 5 minutes, stirring occasionally. Stir in **marshmallows and cherry chips**.

Spread in 8 or 9" square pan which has been lined with wax paper.

Melt **chocolate with peanut butter** in a small pan over low heat, stirring occasionally.

Stir in **peanuts. Spread evenly over cherry layer**.

Let set in refrigerator. Cut into 1" squares.
This fudge reminds me of the cherry mash candy bars.

CHERRY VANILLA FUDGE

1/2 cup **granulated sugar**
1/2 cup dairy **sour cream**
1/3 cup **light corn syrup**
2 tbsp **butter**
1/4 tsp **salt**
2 tsp **vanilla**
1/2 cup diced **candied cherries**
1 cup coarsely **chopped walnuts**

Time - 25 min.

In glass medium bowl, **combine sugar, sour cream, corn syrup, butter** and **salt**.

Microwave at high for 5 minutes. Stir until **sugar** dissolves. Microwave at High 6 minutes or just until mixture reaches **236 degree**s. (Soft ball). Let stand 15 minutes without stirring.

Add **vanilla**; beat until it loses its gloss (about 6 minutes). Stir in **cherries and walnuts**.

Quickly pour in buttered baking dish. Cool. Cut into squares. Makes approximately 1-1/2 pounds.

CHUNKY MALLOW FUDGE

1 cup **crunchy peanut butter**
1 package (12 ounce) **chocolate chips**
4 cups **miniature marshmallows**

Time - 25 min.

Melt together **peanut butter and chocolate chips** in microwave.

Stir and allow to cool slightly (so as not to melt **marshmallows**).

In large bowl, pour **chocolate mixture over marshmallows**.

Stir until **marshmallows** are completely coated.

Pour into **buttered** pan and chill.

COCONUT BUTTER FUDGE

1 1/3 cup **coconut butter**
1/2 cup **honey**
6 tbsp **milk**
4 drops red **food coloring**

Blend **all ingredients** in a food processor.

Press into a wax paper sprayed with **cooking spray 9x13 pan.**

Refrigerate for at least an hour before cutting and serving.

Homemade Coconut Butter

5 oz **unsweetened coconut flakes** or shreds
1 tbsp , melted
1/2 tsp **salt**
1/2 tsp **almond or vanilla extrac**t (optional)

Combine **coconut flake**s in the bowl of a food processor, **add the other ingredients.**

Turn the food processor on high and check after 5 minutes. Scrape sides down into bowl. Then check it again every 5 minutes, for 15 minutes. You know it's done when it starts to stick together like a cookie dough or is beginning to liquify. It will solidify when it cools.

Cool. Store in air tight container at room temperature.

COFFEE FUDGE

2 cups **sugar**
1 cup strong **black coffee**
2 tbsp **heavy cream**
1/2 cup chopped **almonds**

Time - 25 min.

Butter 8" square pan.

Combine **all ingredients** in a heavy pan and boil for 8 minutes (to soft ball stage -- **234F**).

If desired, add **nuts**. Beat until smooth and creamy; pour into pan.

Cool, cut into squares.

COOKIES N CREME WHITE CHOCOLATE FUDGE

1 cup **sugar**
3/4 cup **butter**
1 (5-oz) can **evaporated milk**
2 (12-oz) packages **white chocolate morsels**
1 (7-oz) jar **marshmallow cream**
3 cups coarsely **crushed cream-filled chocolate sandwich cookies**
Pinch of **salt**

Time - 20 min.

Line a greased 9" square pan with aluminum foil; set aside.

Combine **first 3 ingredients** in a medium saucepan. Cook over medium-high heat, stirring constantly, until mixture comes to a boil; cook 3 minutes, stirring constantly. Remove from heat; **add white chocolate morsels, marshmallow cream, 2 cups crushed cookies, and salt**. Stir until morsels melt.

Pour fudge into prepared pan. **Sprinkle remaining 1 cup cookies over fudge**, gently pressing cookies into fudge. Cover and chill until firm (about 1 to 2 hours).

Lift uncut fudge in aluminum foil from pan; remove foil, and cut fudge into square

CRACKER FUDGE

approximately **50 saltine crackers**
1/2 cup **butter**
1 cup **brown sugar**
1 cup **chocolate chips** (white, dark, milk, semisweet or mixture**)**

Time - 30 min.

Preheat oven to **350 degrees**.

Line a jelly roll pan or cookie sheet with aluminum foil.

Layer tightly placed **saltine crackers** on top of foil.

Melt **butter** in saucepan. Add **brown sugar** and stir over medium heat until it forms thick syrup.

Pour syrup evenly over **crackers**.

Spread with a spatula to be sure all **crackers** are coated with syrup.

Bake for 15 minutes. These will burn easily.

Sprinkle **chocolate chips** over **hot crackers** and let stand for 2 minutes until **chocolate chips** are melted enough to spread.

Lightly spread the **chips** with a spatula or knife until there is a smooth coating of chocolate.

Chill until hard.

CRANBERRY FUDGE

1 package **fresh cranberries** (12 oz)
1/2 cup **light corn syrup**
2 cup **white chocolate chips**
1/2 cup **confectioners sugar**
1/4 cup **evaporated milk**
1 tsp **vanilla extract**
1/2 cup **walnuts or pecans** chopped

Time - 25 min. + cooling

Line the bottom and sides of an 8-inch square pan with wax paper sprayed with **cooking spray**. Set aside.

Bring **cranberries and corn syrup** to a boil on high for 5 to 7 minutes, in medium sauce pan.
Stirring until the liquid is reduced to about 3 tbsp. remove from heat.

Mix in **chocolate chips** and stir until they are melted.

Mix in **confectioners sugar, evaporated milk, vanilla extract and nuts.** Whip with wooden spoon until the mixture is thick and glossy.

Pour into the pan. Cover and chill until firm.

EGGNOG WHITE CHOCOLATE FUDGE

2 cups **sugar**
1/2 cup **butter**
3/4 cup **dairy eggnog**
3 (3 1/2 oz) packages **white chocolate**, broken into pieces
1/2 tsp grated **nutmeg**
1 (7 ounce) jar **marshmallow creme**
1 cup chopped **pecans**
1 tsp **rum extract**

Time - 30 min.

Combine **sugar, butter and eggnog** in a heavy 2-1/2 to 3 quart saucepan; bring to a full boil, stirring constantly.

Continue boiling until a candy thermometer reaches **234 degrees** F, stirring constantly to prevent scorching.

Remove from heat; stir in **white chocolate pieces and nutmeg** until chocolate is melted.

Add **marshmallow creme, nuts and rum extract**. Beat until well blended.

Pour into **buttered** 8 or 9 inch square pan.

Chill fudge; cut into squares.

FUDGE 1894

3 cups of **brown sugar**,
Just enough **cream to wet the sugar**,
1 pinch of **salt**,
1 pinch of **soda**,
1 tsp of **vanilla**,
1/2 cup **Butter**,
1/3 cup of **chocolate**.

Time - 20 min.

Stir the **cream** well into the **sugar**; then place it on the stove. Watch carefully, so it cannot burn; then, when it begins to boil, add **salt and soda**. Later, put in the **chocolate and butter**.

Take it off before it is quite done; then add the **vanilla**. Beat it until it creams; then pour in a dish. Cool and cut in squares.

My Grandmother's notes: This was taken from a Cookbook before the 1900's.

GRANDPAS FAMOUS PEANUT BUTTER FUDGE

2 cups packed **brown sugar**
3/4 cup **milk** (or 1 5-oz can evaporated milk)
3/4 stick **butter**
1 tsp **vanilla**
chopped nuts (optional)
1 cup **peanut butter**

Time - 25 min.

Butter pan or plate, set aside.

Combine in sauce pan, **brown sugar and milk**.

Mix in pan and heat to "soft ball stage" or **240 degrees** on candy thermometer.

Remove from heat and add **butter, vanilla, chopped nuts and peanut butter**.

Beat, and then pour into prepared pan.

Refrigerate. Cut into squares.

GUMDROP WHITE CHOCOLATE FUDGE

1 1/2 lbs. **white candy coating, coarsely chopped or white chocolate chips**.
1 (14 oz) can **sweetened condensed milk**
1/8 tsp **salt**
1 1/2 tsp **vanilla extract**
1 1/2 cups **chopped gumdrops**

Time - 20 min.

Line a 9-in. square pan with foil, and spray with **cooking spray**; set aside.

In a large saucepan, heat the **candy coating or white chocolate, milk and salt** over low heat until coating is melted. Remove from the heat; stir in **vanilla and gumdrops**.

Spread into prepared pan. Cover and refrigerate until firm.

Remove fudge from the pan; cut into 1-in. squares. Makes about 3 pounds.

IRISH CREAM FUDGE

4 cups (500g) **dark chocolate melts**
1 can (395g) **sweetened condensed milk**
60g butter = 4 tbsp **Butter**
1/4 cup (65ml) **Irish cream liqueur**

Time - 30 min.

Line a baking sheet with wax paper and set aside.

Place the **chocolate, condensed milk and butter** in a small saucepan. Stir continuously over a low heat until the chocolate is melted.

Remove saucepan from heat and whisk in **Irish cream liqueur**.

Pour into baking sheet and refrigerate for 3-4 hours or until set. Cut into squares.

Vary this fudge by varying the flavor of liqueur. **Tia Maria or Kahlua** for coffee flavor or **Crème de Menthe** for minty chocolate fudge.

KAHLUA FUDGE

1 1/3 cup **granulated sugar**
1 jar (7oz) **marshmallow cream**
2/3 cup **evaporated milk**
1/4 cup **butter**
2 cup **semi-swee**t chocolate chips
1 cup **milk chocolate chips**
2/3 cup **walnuts**, chopped
1 tsp **vanilla**
1/4 cup **Kahlua liquor**

Time - 25 min. + cooling

Line 8" square baking pan with foil and spray with **cooking spray**.

Combine **sugar, marshmallow cream, milk, butter & Kahlua** in medium sauce pan. Bring to rapid boil, stirring constantly for 5 minutes.

Remove from heat, add **all chips** and stir till melted. Add **nuts and vanilla**.

Turn onto prepared pan. Refrigerate until firm, cut into squares.

LEMON FUDGE

1-1/2 tsp plus 6 tbsp **butter**, divided
2 packages (10 to 12 oz each) **vanilla or white chips**
2/3 cup **sweetened condensed milk**
2/3 cup **marshmallow creme**
1-1/2 tsp **lemon extract**

Time - 25 min. + cooling

Line a 9-in. square pan with foil. Grease foil with **1-1/2 tsp butter;** set aside

Melt remaining butter in medium sauce pan over low heat. Mix in **chips and milk;** cook and stir for 10 min. or until chips are melted.

Stir in **marshmallow creme and extract**; continue to cook and stirring 3-4 minutes longer or until smooth.

Pour into prepared pan. Chill until set.

Using foil, lift fudge out of pan, and cut into squares. Store in the refrigerator. Yield: about 2 pounds.

MACA COCONUT FUDGE

1 cup **coconut oil**, melted
3 tbsp **raw cacao powder**
1/4 cup **maple syrup**
1 tsp **vanilla extract**
1 tsp **maca powder**
1/2 tsp **cinnamon**
1/4 cup **unsweetened shredded coconut**
1 pinch **sea salt** for sprinkling on top
cacao powder for top, optional

Time - 1 hour & 10 min.

Melt **coconut oil and mix with cacao powder, maple syrup, vanilla extract, maca powder, cinnamon and shredded coconut.**

Line 8×8 baking dish with wax paper and spray with **cooking spray**. Pour **mixture into dish**.

Sprinkle **sea salt and additional cacao powder** over the top (if using).

Refrigerate about 1 hour, until set, then slice and serve.

Store in the refrigerator in air tight container and eat within a few days.

Notes: We have used **stevia**, but use 1 1/2 tbsp and reduce the maple syrup. Please note that **cacao powder** is different than **cocoa powder**, but cocoa powder can also be used in this recipe.

MAPLE FUDGE

3 cups **maple syrup**
1 cup **milk**
1/2 cup **chopped nuts**

Time - 20 min.

Put **maple syrup and milk** in heavy saucepan.

Boil mixture to the soft ball stage, **236 degrees** on the candy thermometer.

Remove from heat, cool to lukewarm.

Beat mixture until creamy. Add **nuts**.

Pour mixture into 8 inch **buttered** square pan. Spread mixture out evenly. Scour with knife.

Let cool until firm. Cut into pieces. Store in airtight container in a cool place. Makes about 16 pieces

MILLION DOLLAR FUDGE

2 (6 oz) pkg **semi-sweet chocolate chips**
4 1/2 cup **sugar**
1 tall can **evaporated milk**
1 1/2 tbsp **butter**
1 pint **marshmallow cream**
2 cup **nuts**
1 tsp **salt**

Time - 20 min.

Bring **sugar, milk, and salt** to a boil and cook 6 minutes. Stirring while cooking.

Mix **remaining ingredients** in large mixing bowl.

Pour boiling mixture over ingredients in bowl. Beat with mixer until melted and thick.

Sets fast. Store in refrigerator.

MINT CHOCOLATE FUDGE

12 oz **bittersweet chocolate**, chopped
3 o **unsweetened chocolate**, chopped
1/2 cup **marshmallow crème**
3 cups **sugar**
1 1/2 tsp **peppermint extract** (be generous)
2/3 cup **water**
1 can **sweetened condensed milk**
2/3 cup **whipping cream**
1/2 cup **unsalted butter**

Time - 25 min.

Line a 9 inch pan with foil or **butter**.

Place **chocolates, marshmallow and peppermint** in bowl. Mix **sugar, milk, water, cream** and **butte**r in a heavy saucepan.

Stir over medium-low heat until **sugar** dissolves. Increase heat to high and bring to a full rolling boil. Reduce heat to medium-high and stir slowly until candy thermometer reaches 235 F.

Pour boiling mixture over ingredients in bowl. Stir vigorously with spoon until chocolate melts and fudge thickens slightly, about 2 minutes.

Immediately pour fudge into prepared pan, smooth top and chill until firm.

ORANGE CHOCOLATE FUDGE

380g (13 oz) **chocolate chips or chocolate drops**
1 can **condensed sweetened milk**
1/2 cup chopped **pecans**
1 tbsp grated **orange zest**
optional - 1/2 tsp **orange flavoring**

Time - 15 min.

Line a 8x8 in. square tin with wax paper.

Melt **chocolate with condensed milk** in a double boiler or in a bowl in the microwave. Stir until smooth. Remove from heat and stir in **pecans** and **grated orange zest and/or flavoring.**

Pour **chocolate mixture** into prepared pan. Chill 2 hours, or until firm, and cut into squares. Store, covered, in the refrigerator.

ORANGE N CREAM FUDGE

6 oz (1.5 sticks) **butter**
2 cups granulated **sugar**
3/4- cup **heavy cream**
1 package (12 oz) **white chocolate chips**
1 jar (7 oz) **marshmallow cream-fluff**
1 tbsp **orange extract**
orange food coloring (or a combination of red and yellow) food coloring

Time - 30 min. + cooling

Prepare a 13x9 pan by lining it with aluminum foil and spraying the foil with **nonstick cooking** spray.

Combine **sugar, cream, and butter** in medium sauce pan over medium heat.

Stirring mixture until the butter melts and the sugar dissolves.

Brush **sugar** off sides of pan with a wet pastry brush.

Bring the **mixture to a boil**, when boiling continue for 4 min.

After boiling, remove pan from the heat, and stir in the **marshmallow cream and white chocolate chips.**

Stirring until white chocolate has melted, and fudge is smooth.

Work fast to pour a third of the white fudge into a bowl and set aside.

Add the **orange extract and orange food coloring** to remaining batch, stirring until it is a smooth, even color. It is very important to work quickly, because fudge will start to set, and it will not be smooth.

Pour **orange fudge into prepared pan** spreading a even layer.

Drop **white fudge by spoonfuls** onto orange fudge and dray a knife or toothpick to create orange-white swirls. Spray your hands with nonstick cooking spray and gently press top to smooth out the swirls.

Set fudge at room temperature for 2 hours, or 1 hour in refrigerator to set.

Pull the fudge out of the pan using the foil as handles, and cut.

To cut the fudge into small 1-inch squares, use a sharp knife . Store in airtight container in the refrigerator for up to a week. Serve at room temperature.

OREO FUDGE

3 cups **white sugar**
3/4 cup **butter**
2/3 cup **evaporated milk**
2 cups **white chocolate chips**
1 (7 oz) **jar marshmallow creme**
1 tsp **vanilla extract**
1/2 cup **crumbled chocolate sandwich cookies** (such as Oreo®)
1 cup **crushed chocolate sandwich cookies** (topping)

Time - 25 min.

Line 13x9-inch baking pan with wax paper and spray with **cooking spray**.
.

Combine sugar, **butter, and evaporated milk** to a boil in saucepan, stirring constantly; cook 3-6 min. until mixture is smooth. Remove saucepan from heat; stir **white chocolate chips** and **marshmallow creme** into sugar mixture until melted. Add **vanilla extract**; stir.

Fold **1/2 cup crumbled cookies** into **white chocolate mixture** until mixed well. Spread into prepared pan. Sprinkle **1 cup crushed cookies** evenly over the top. Press cookies lightly into the fudge.

Cool at room temperature until set. Cut into small squares. Store in tight covered container in refrigerator.

PEANUT BUTTER FUDGE

1 package **white almond bark**
1 cup **peanut butter**
1 cup semi-sweet **chocolate chips**

Time - 15 min.

Melt **all 3 ingredients** together in microwave until melted together.

Pour into a 9" square pan that has been lined (up the sides) with wax paper.

Let set till it hardens**.**

PEANUT SOUR CREAM FUDGE

4 cups **sugar**
1 cup (8 ounces) **sour cream**
2/3 cup **light corn syrup**
1/4 cup **butter**
1/2 tsp **salt**
1 tbsp vanilla extract
1 cup **chopped peanuts**
2/3 cup **peanut butter**

Time - 15 min + cooling

In saucepan, combine the **first five ingredients**; bring to a boil. Cover, simmer for 5 minutes.

Uncover; cook over medium-high heat until a candy thermometer reads **238°** (soft-ball stage).

Remove from heat; add **vanilla**. Let stand, without stirring, for 15 minutes.

Add **peanuts and peanut butter**. Beat with wooden spoon until thick and creamy, about 10 minutes.

Transfer to buttered 13-in. x 9-in. pan or slab. Cool; cut squares. Store in the refrigerator.

Yield: 3 pounds.

PECAN DATE FUDGE

3/4 cup **butter**
3 cups granulated **sugar**
2/3 cup **evaporated milk**
1/2 cup **chopped dates**
12 oz **white candy coating or white chocolate**
4 cups mini **marshmallows**
1 cup chopped **pecans**
1 tsp **vanilla extract**

Time - 25 min.

In a heavy pan, combine the **butter, sugar, and milk.** Cook and stir over low heat till **sugar** is dissolved, bring to a boil, boil and stir for 4 minutes.

Add **dates**, boil and stir for 1 min. remove from heat, stir in **candy coating** and **marshmallows,** until melted, beat till smooth.

Add **pecans and vanilla,** beat with wooden spoon till glossy

Pour into **buttered** 13x9 pan.

Cool and cut into squares.

PECAN PIE FUDGE

1 **pie crust**
1 1/2 cups **pecan halves**, coarsely chopped
1/2 cup **dark corn syrup**
1/3 cup **evaporated milk**
3 cups **white chocolate chips**
1/2 cup **brown sugar**
1 tsp **vanilla extract**
1/4 tsp **maple extract**

Time - 45 min + cooling

Preheat oven to **400F. Line a 8x8" or 9x9"** pan with foil and spray with **cooking spray.**

Place **pecans on a baking sheet** and toast lightly in the oven. Watch closely for 1 min., do not burn. Open the oven and gently shake the pan. Pecans are ready when you smell them.

Unroll pie crust, cut an 8x8 square. Place in pan and poke with fork several times. **Bake for 10-12 minutes** until the crust is golden around the edges.

When crust comes out of oven, set aside. In medium sauce pan over medium low heat combine **corn syrup, evaporated milk, white chocolate chips, and brown sugar**. Stirring until mixture is melted and smooth. Remove heat, stir in **vanilla and maple extract.**

Pour over **hot crust**. Top with **pecans** and press down, so that all the **pecans** are touching the fudge.

Cool fudge firm. Cools in refrigerator faster. Can be stored at room temperature, sealed in a container.

PANUCHE FUDGE

butter flavored oil **cooking spray**
1 can (5 oz) **evaporated milk**
1 1/2 cups packed **light-brown sugar**
5 oz (1 1/4 sticks) **butter**
1/4 tsp **salt**
1/2 cup **powdered sugar**
1 tsp **vanilla extract**
3 oz - 1 cup toasted **walnuts** (or **pecans**) chopped

Time - 20 min.

Coat a 5-by-10-inch loaf pan with cooking spray. Line with wax paper leaving a 2-inch overhang on 2 sides.

Bring **evaporated milk, brown sugar, butter, and salt** to a boil in a medium saucepan, stirring constantly. Reduce heat to medium-low, stirring frequently, until mixture registers **236 degrees**. About 25 minutes.

Remove from heat and whip until smooth. Pour into prepared pan.

PINA COLADA FUDGE

1 (12 oz) package **white chocolate chips**
1 (16 oz) tub **cream cheese or vanilla frosting**
1/4 tsp **salt**
1/2 tsp **rum extract**
1/2 cup **dried pineapple**, chopped
1/4 cup **toasted flaked coconut**
1/3 cup **chopped macadamia nuts**
1/3 cup **chopped pecans**
more **nuts or fruit for garnish** (optional)

Time - 30 min + cooling

Butter an 8 x 8-inch baking pan or a 9-inch diameter pan. Set aside.

Melt the **baking chips in the microwave** in a medium bowl.

Stir in the **frosting, salt, extract, nuts and fruit** until well combined.

Scrape into the prepared pan and **sprinkle with additional nuts or fruit as garnish,** if using.

Refrigerate for at least 1/2 hour or until firm. Cut it into squares to serve.

NOTE: *I used a silicone pan, so I skipped step one and it made popping out the fudge so easy.

PISTACHIO IRISH CREME FUDGE

36 oz (3 bags) **white chocolate chips**
1 14 oz can **sweetened condense milk**
1/2 cup **Irish cream liquor**
1/2 cup **raw pistachios**

Time - 25 min. + Cooling

Line a square 8x8 pan with wax paper sprayed with cooking spray.

Mix **all ingredients, except pistachios** in medium sauce pan over medium heat. Stirring often until **chocolate** has almost melted. Being careful not to burn.

Remove heat and continue stirring until **chocolate is melted**. **Add pistachios,** pour evenly onto prepared pan.

Let cool until set. Remove fudge from pan and cut into small squares. Store in air tight container in refrigerator. Serve room temperature.

PRALINE PECAN FUDGE

12 oz **evaporated milk**
1 1/2 cups **sugar**
1/4 cup **butter**
1/2 tsp **cinnamon**
1/2 tsp **salt**
1 tsp **vanilla extract**
1 1/2 cups **pecans**

Time - 25 min. + cooling

Combine **milk, sugar, salt, and cinnamon** (equal parts of cream and sugar if you are adding to recipe). In medium sauce pan over medium heat.

Boil until thermometer reaches **210F** and **add butter and vanilla.**

When temperature reaches **soft ball stage 235 degrees**, add **1-1/2 cups pecans.**

When temperature reaches 2 degrees higher, remove heat, **whip fudge** until glossy and feels heavy.

Spoon onto **buttered platter.**

Allow to cool. Store covered in air tight container.

PUMPKIN FUDGE

3/4 cup unsalted **butter**
3 cups **sugar**
2/3 cup **evaporated milk**
1 cup canned **pumpkin**
2 tbsp **light corn syrup**
2 1/2 tsp **pumpkin pie spice**
9 oz **white chocolate chips**
7 oz **marshmallow fluff**
1 tsp **vanilla extract**

Time - 25 min.

Melt **butter** in a medium saucepan over medium heat.

Increasing heat to medium high, stir in the **sugar, milk, pumpkin, corn syrup**, and **pumpkin pie spice**.

Cook, stirring constantly, until mixture comes to a boil. Continue cooking, stirring constantly, until a candy thermometer at **234 degrees** F (soft-ball stage).

Remove pan from heat. Stir in **white chocolate, marshmallow fluff, and vanilla** until blended well.

Line a 9x9 baking dish with aluminum foil and lightly coat with **cooking spray**. Spread fudge into the dish. Refrigerate until completely cool. Cut fudge into squares

Melt in your mouth pumpkin pie, white chocolate taste.

RASPBERRY FUDGE BALLS

1 package (8 oz) **cream cheese,** softened
1 package (6 oz) **semi-sweet chocolate chips**, melted
3/4 cup **vanilla wafer crumbs**
1/4 cup **raspberry preserves**, strained
1/3 cup finely chopped **almonds**
Powdered sugar

Time - 20 min.

Combine **cream cheese and chocolate**, mixing until well blended.

Stir in **crumbs and preserves**.

Chill.

Shape into 1 inch balls; roll in **almonds and powdered sugar**.

Chill several hours.

ROCKY ROAD FUDGE

2 tbs **butter**
1 (12 oz) pkg **semi-sweet chocolate chip**s
1 (14 oz) can **Eagle Brand milk**
2 cup dry **roasted peanuts**
1 (10 1/2 oz) pkg **miniature marshmallows**

Time - 20 min. + cooling

Melt **chocolate morsels with Eagle Brand and 2 tbs butter**, in sauce pan.

Remove from heat, add **peanuts and marshmallows**. Stir thoroughly and spread onto waxed paper-lined and sprayed with butter cooking spray, 13 x 9 inch pan. Chill 2 hours

SANTA'S WHITE FUDGE

2 cups **sugar**
1/2 cup **sour cream**
1/3 cup **white corn syrup**
2 tbsp **butter**
1/4 tsp **salt**
2 tsp **vanilla**
1/4 cup **candied cherries**, chopped
1 cup **pecans**, chopped

Time - 20 min.

In large heavy skillet, (medium sauce pan) mix **first 5 ingredients**; cook to softball stage.

Remove from heat; let stand 15 minutes.

Add **vanilla** and beat; add **cherries and nuts**.

Pour into buttered 8x8 inch pan.

SPICED PUMPKIN FUDGE

3 cups **sugar**
3/4 cups **butter**
2/3 cups **evaporated milk**
1/2 cup canned **pumpkin**
1 tsp **pumpkin pie spice**
1 package (12 oz) **butterscotch morsels**
1 jar (7 oz) **marshmallow crème**
1 cup chopped toasted **almonds**
1 tsp **vanilla**

Time - 20 min.

Butter a 13x9 inch cake pan, set aside.

In a heavy saucepan, combine the **sugar, butter, milk, pumpkin** and **spice**.

Bring to a boil, stirring constantly; continue to boil over a medium heat stirring constantly until mixture reaches 234 degrees on a candy thermometer, about 10 minutes.

Remove from heat and stir in **butterscotch morsels**; add **marshmallow crème, nuts** and **vanilla**, mixing until blended.

STRAWBERRY FUDGE

2 cups **sugar**
1 cup **preserved strawberries**
1/2 cup **water**
2 egg **whites (stiffly beaten)**
1/4 tsp **cream of tartar**

Time - 30 min.

Boil **sugar, water, and cream of tartar** to firm ball stage (248 F).

Add **strawberries** which have been drained as dry as possible. Let come to a boil again.

Pour slowly, beating constantly, over **stiffly beaten egg whites**. Beat until thick and fluffy.

Pour into well-**buttered** pans. When firm cut in squares. Any **thick preserves** or **candied fruit** may be substituted for strawberries.

SUNSHINE LIME FUDGE

3 cups **white baking pieces**
1 14 - oz can (1-1/4 cups) **sweetened condensed milk**
2 tsp finely shredded **lime peel**
2 tsp **fresh Key lime juice**, or bottled lime juice
1 cup **chopped macadamia nuts**, toasted if desired

Time - 20 mins. + cooling

Line an 8x8x2- or 9x9x2-inch baking pan with wax paper sprayed with **cooking oil**. Set aside.

Mix **baking pieces and sweetened condensed milk,** in medium sauce pan over low heat until smooth. Remove from heat. Stir in **lime peel and lime juice**. Stir in **macadamia nuts.**

Spread mixture evenly into prepared pan. Sprinkle a few additional coarsely chopped **macadamia nuts** over the top. Cover and chill until firm.

Remove fudge from pan. Cut into pieces. Store in an airtight container at room temperature for up to 1 week or in the freezer for up to 2 months. Makes 2 pounds fudge.

Note: I have sprinkled this fudge with homemade lime flavored sugar with green food color mixed in. Also added a few drops of green food coloring into fudge for St. Patrick's Day Fudge.

VANILLA FUDGE

2 cups **sugar**
5-oz can **evaporated milk**
1/3 cup **milk**
1/8 tsp **salt**
1/4 cup **butter**
1 tsp **vanilla extract**
chopped **nuts** (optional)

Time - 25 min.

Line an 8x4x2-inch loaf pan with foil, extending foil over edges of pan. **Butter** foil, set aside.

Butter the sides of a heavy 2-quart saucepan. In saucepan combine **sugar, evaporated milk, milk, and salt**. Cook and stir over medium-high heat to boiling.

Cook and stir over medium-low-heat to **238 degrees**, soft-ball stage (this should take 25 to 35 minutes).

Immediately remove saucepan from heat. Add **butter and vanilla**, but do not stir. Cool mixture, without stirring, to **110 degrees**, lukewarm (about 55 minutes).

Remove candy thermometer from saucepan. Beat vigorously with a wooden spoon till fudge becomes very thick and just starts to lose its gloss (about 10 minutes total). Do not over beat.

Immediately spread fudge into the prepared pan. Score into 1-inch squares while warm. Top each square with a **piece of nut**, if desired.

When candy is firm, use the foil to lift the fudge out of the pan. Cut into squares. Store, tightly covered, in the refrigerator. Makes 1 lb.

WALNUT MAPLE FUDGE

2 tbsp **butter**
2/3 cup evaporated **milk**
1-1/2 cup **granulated sugar**
1/4 tsp **salt**
2 cups (4 oz) **miniature marshmallows**
2 cups (12 oz package) **white chocolate chips**
1/2 cup chopped **walnuts**
1-1/2 tsp **maple extract**
chopped **walnuts** (optional**)**

Time - 20 min.

Combine **butter, evaporated milk, sugar and salt** in medium, heavy duty saucepan. Bring to a full rolling boil, stirring constantly, over medium heat. Boil, stirring constantly for 4-1/2 to 5 minutes.

Remove from heat. Stir in **marshmallows, white chocolate chip morsels, nuts** and **maple flavoring**. Stir vigorously for 1 minute or until **marshmallow**s are melted.

Pour into **buttered** 13x9 inch baking pan. Cool until firm. Cut into squares. Makes about 50 pieces.

About the Authors

COUNTRY SISTERS GOURMET - Co-creators Alice Turner and Carol Vaughn are sisters who were raised on a family spice farm in southeastern Arizona. These "country sisters" teamed up to give you some of their best recipes. In their books you will get a wide variety from old recipes that have been passed along, to their modern day dishes. Some of these have been used and passed on from their grandmothers, their mother Laura, and many other family members and friends.

Alice still doesn't consider herself grown up, but when she married and left the family spice farm...*many* years ago, she moved to southwest New Mexico where she continued to farm with her husband, David. On the farm, Alice not only had access to the commercial crops, but she was blessed to having her acre plus gardens planted in the nearest "field". She has always been known for her delicious cooking and baking and had the resources to use fresh, home grown ingredients. Alice has since moved off of the farm, but she took her "country cooking" skills with her! She expanded her culinary knowledge by studying and took on new interests in catering and party planning. She still delights her family and friends with her favorite recipes and meals and is always trying new ideas. Alice now spends her time quilting, gardening, canning, cooking, baking, and enjoying her grandchildren.

Carol moved from the family spice farm to a ranch in southwestern New Mexico. It was then that this cowgirl figured out that if she would get off of her horse now and then...she could be really good in the kitchen too! She enjoyed being creative with old recipes and came up with some great dishes. She favors making desserts, baking breads, and cooking dishes using fresh produce from her garden. Carol's cooking skills expanded as she prepared meals for many guests and the cowboys on the ranch. Carol is still a cowgirl and enjoys riding and training her horses, but she also finds the time to enjoy writing, painting, photography, spending time with family and friends and traveling. Her collections are memoirs from her childhood years on the spice farm to her many years of ranching.

You can enjoy these recipes for yourself in their books from... Country Sisters Gourmet!

Printed in Great Britain
by Amazon